from
Self-Care
to **Prayer**

31 REFRESHING

SPIRITUAL TIPS

Gary Egeberg

TWENTY-THIRD PUBLICATIONS

Mystic, CT 06355

Gary Egeberg facilitates workshops, classes, and retreats on spirituality, prayer, and emotional health. He can be reached by email at gary.egeberg2@gte.net

Twenty-Third Publications
185 Willow Street
P.O. Box 180
Mystic, CT 06355
(860) 536-2611
(800) 321-0411

ISBN: 0-89622-980-7
Library of Congress Catalog Card Number: 99-70820
Printed in the U.S.A.

"Gary Egeberg has done a masterful job of condensing a wealth of wisdom into a simple format. I especially liked the helps at the end of each chapter to aid the reader to integrate the insights presented. I'll be giving this book to many of my clients."

Earnie Larsen, M.R.E.
Author, *Days of Healing, Days of Joy*

"Anyone seeking personal health and holiness will find this book a helpful 'beginner's guide' for their journey. *From Self-Care to Prayer* is more than a self-help book, however. Gary Egeberg has provided a pathway to *spiritual* refreshment and a way to tap into the power of God."

Bill Huebsch
Author, *A New Look at Prayer: Searching for Bliss*

"Gary Egeberg's spiritual tips are indeed refreshing for those of us who all too easily forget about the unconditional nature of God's love, grace, and encouragement. *From Self-Care to Prayer* presents an insightful, kind antidote to our negativity and spiritual stagnation. These tips are very helpful for my own journey."

Terry D. Cooper, Ed.D.
Author, *I'm Judgmental, You're Judgmental*
and *Accepting the Troll Underneath the Bridge*

"In his book, *From Self-Care to Prayer*, Gary Egeberg has succeeded where many spiritual self-help books fall short. In a series of brief but practical 'tips,' he has shaped a personal way of interfacing familiar situations of stress and emotional challenges with authentic biblical sources and a genuinely God-centered spirituality."

Fr. John Heagle
Co-director of Therapy and Renewal Associates
Adjunct professor, School of Theology and Ministry, Seattle University

"Praying over Egeberg's insightful tips—seeing anger as a friend; judging ourselves by progress, not perfection; accepting God's unconditional love; finding strengths in our weaknesses; facing our fears; forgiving ourselves; finding serenity in surrender to God—may lead us to more human prayer and increasing intimacy with God. Being more open with ourselves, we become more open with God and converse as lovers should.

"Human psychology and spirituality intersect, as they should, in this detailed and practical volume on prayer. The pray-er can move about these pages with ease, discovering what touches the heart and pausing where fruitful."

John G. van Bemmel
Author, *Prayers about Everyday Stuff: Off the Cuff and from the Heart*
Co-Author, *100 Prayers for Making Faith Connections*

"Although the author and I have never met, I read this book as if it were written directly for me and my friends. It will become part of my meditations and gift-giving this year. Practical! Practical! Practical! Eminently practical suggestions for those who desire oneness with God even in a busy life."

Virginia Ann Froehle, R.S.M.
Retreat and spiritual director
Author, *Loving Yourself More: 101 Meditations for Women*

"*From Self-Care to Prayer* is inspirational, motivating, and practical. The user-friendly format provides options for the reader to select particular 'Spiritual Tips' depending on circumstance, desire, or need. The easy reading style offers wonderful tools for deepening one's spirituality while utilizing the information as it fits into your lifestyle.

"The spiritual tips, practical applications, and affirmations can be a source for individual prayer and spiritual growth as well as for creating group prayer and rituals. Egeberg offers a resource that combines self-care with God's care that can be used again and again...an asset to anyone's book collection."

Barbara Schwery
National BeFriender Ministry Trainer and Consultant
The Saint Paul Seminary School of Divinity, University of St. Thomas

Dedication

For my wife Peggy, who is a wonderful answer to prayer
and whose generous love, faithful support,
and timely wisdom are essential to my self-care

Acknowledgments

I would like to thank my editors at Twenty-Third Publications: Debbie McCann, for her initial work on the manuscript; Lisa Wilson, for her supportive words and enthusiasm; and Lisa Coleman, for her friendliness and patience as we worked on the finishing touches.

Thank you to my wife, Peggy, for being my first "editor" and for honestly sharing your opinions about the various tips with me—even though I sometimes responded to your feedback like a recalcitrant grouch rather than a grateful partner.

I extend loving gratitude to my parents, Thelma and Ruben Egeberg, for being co-creators with God in giving me the gift of life—painful as it is sometimes—and for your faithful love and support.

Thank you to my sister, Donna Marcue, for sharing the ups and downs of those early years of recovery with me and for the many ways you helped me from the very first tentative day of the journey to wholeness. And, I say thank you to my brother, Dale Egeberg, for being there for me during a very painful period in my life, and for the wonderful conversations we have had over the years.

Finally, I would like to express gratitude to each of the members of my Friday night Twelve-Step group whose support, wisdom, and friendship are gifts of immeasurable value.

Contents

From Self-Care to Prayer

Introduction

Most of us, no matter what phase or stage of adulthood we find ourselves in, lead very busy, stressful, tiring lives. We often face a plateful of time-consuming and energy-draining responsibilities that include earning a living, commuting, obtaining additional schooling or training, spending time with family and friends, as well as many others. We may be stretched to the limit out of necessity or because we have a hard time saying no to those who make demands of us or because staying busy is the only path we know. Because we are so busy, it can be increasingly difficult for many of us to sense God's presence in our lives. The faster and fuller our lives are the harder it is to slow down and empty ourselves for a few minutes so that we can more readily receive what God desires to give us. Whatever the causes of our busyness, it's important that we remember to take care of ourselves. Doing so can make all the difference between being extended and overextended, tired and fatigued, or stressed and stressed-out.

Not only does the fast-paced and full lifestyle many of us lead contribute to feeling stressed and disconnected from God, each other, and ourselves but so do the problems and difficulties we encounter in daily life. Struggling with painful emotions, experiencing conflicts at home or work, and suffering from perfectionism are just a few of the many issues that can take their toll upon our spirits and which call for self-care and prayer.

This book offers a variety of simple, practical, and satisfying ways to combine self-care with God's care. For example, it can be very de-stressing and refreshing to pause for thirty seconds while at work or when stuck in a traffic jam and prayerfully repeat the phrase "God is with me" over and over. Or, at the end of an exhausting day or week, it can be spiritually and physically renewing to simply lie on your bed with pillows under your knees and head and allow yourself to sink into God's tender care.

The thirty-one spiritual "tips" in this book are intended to offer a few practical and doable suggestions for praying and caring for ourself in the midst of a variety of common human experiences, ranging from coping with fears and resentments to celebrating personal progress and expressing gratitude. Each tip begins with some introductory thoughts for you to consider under the heading, *About this spiritual tip,* which is followed by a few suggestions for putting the particular tip into practice in a section entitled *Applying and Activating.* Most of the tips close with the heading, *Affirmations and Truths,* which consists of a variety of positive statements that can be used for meditation, reflection, or as an entryway to prayer, while a handful of tips close with an additional exercise you might consider trying. Across from these, you will find a blank page for writing your own thoughts, prayers, or affirmations if you are inclined to do so.

The tips are not meant to be read in order, nor are they intended to serve as spiritual reading for a month. Instead, you are invited to use the Contents page to locate one that might be helpful on a particular day for a particular situation you are facing. Or you may just want to browse through the book and read whatever catches your eye. The tips are just that: tips, ideas, suggestions, which you are welcome to explore, tweak, or ignore.

I wrote this book not because I have mastered either self-care or prayer, but because I need to practice both continually. I frequently lose my way in prayer and often go through much of my day unaware of God's presence. Like many people, I experience stress, struggle with anger from time to time, resist fear, and dread conflicts. This book may be helpful to those who, like me, find a few of the following statements to be true for them:

- if you are a young adult, not-so-young adult, or an older adult
- if you get crabby once in a while (in other words if you are a parent)
- if you occasionally or regularly get stressed-out or upset in traffic
- if you have a hunger for God and want to draw closer to God
- if you want to pray but don't have a lot of time or find prayer to be unsatisfying
- if you are in a Twelve-Step program or used to be in a Twelve-Step program
- if you are a Christian or belong to another faith tradition or no faith tradition
- if you sometimes struggle with loneliness, sadness, guilt, or shame
- if you want some ideas for coping with anger, resentments, and conflict
- if you tend to be hard on yourself when you fail or make mistakes
- if you long to experience self-acceptance and God's acceptance more often
- if you want to discover some simple ways to connect with God during your day

It is my hope that some of the "tips" will be truly refreshing and helpful for you or the person for whom you are considering this book. It is my further hope that a few might serve as springboards for greater self-care and deeper prayer.

Gary Egeberg

Spiritual Tips and Affirmations

I AM
loved,
lovable,
and
loving

Self-Affirmations

About this spiritual tip: Some of us suffer from a harsh inner voice that criticizes our every move. What we do and who we are are never good enough for the inner critic. When this cruel voice dominates, not only does our self-worth diminish, but any sense of being unconditionally loved by God disappears as well. But, we do not have to be passive and allow the critical voice to go unchallenged. We can—and must!—affirm and fight for ourselves. We might not initially believe the positive words we speak to and about ourselves, but we can choose to speak them again and again, confident that our God will help us believe the unalterable truth that we *are* good people. Gradually the vociferous inner critical voice will decrease and a gentler voice of self-love will increase.

Applying and Activating

- Slowly and prayerfully read the list of affirmations two or more times.
- Read the list aloud so as to hear the words of truth being spoken in addition to seeing them.
- Pause for a few seconds between each affirmation and allow

the healing words to penetrate your heart and mind and decrease the power of the inner critical voice.

◆ Read one or two affirmations that you resonate with the most over and over

◆ Consider writing additional affirmations on the lines provided.

Self-Affirmations

I am a creative person made in the Creator's image

I am a thoughtful, kind, and compassionate person

I accept myself at all times and treat myself gently—especially when I am hurting

I am loved, lovable, and loving

I totally forgive myself for all my mistakes and failings

I am changing and growing in many positive ways

I am proud of who I am and of the ways I contribute to my family, friends, and work

I have the personal power to make healthy choices on my behalf

I choose to treat myself with great tenderness at this very moment

My thoughts, prayers, or affirmations

_____

_____

_____

_____

_____

_____

_____

_____

_____

_____

_____

_____

_____

I love you
as
you are
at
this moment

God-Affirmations

About this spiritual tip: God "speaks" positive and affirming words to each one of us, but too often we are unable to hear, much less receive, these words of loving acceptance. Perhaps important people—adults or peers—during our childhood years were overly critical of us, thus making it difficult for us to experience God's love. Receivers of criticism, many of us have become senders of criticism—to ourselves and others.

God's voice of unconditional love, however, dwells within us and desires to be heard. We can activate this voice and speak God's words of affirmation to ourselves in God's voice, much like the biblical prophets spoke for God. All we need do is open to the inner voice of love.

Applying and Activating

- ◆ Slowly and prayerfully read the list of affirmations two or three times.
- ◆ Close your eyes and repeat one affirmation over and over and imagine it sinking deeper into your heart.
- ◆ Identify the most powerful critical messages that are still

crippling you today and create affirmations in God's voice to counteract them.

◆ Write an affirming letter to yourself in God's voice and allow God to tell you how much you are loved and valued as you are.

God-Affirmations

I love you *as you are* at this very moment

I love you and accept you completely and unconditionally

When you make a poor choice, I am here to help you and forgive you

Nothing can separate you from my love

As my beloved child, I will always hold you and help you

I am with you at each and every moment and will never abandon you

I want you to know peace and happiness

Gently set aside self-criticism and allow my love to heal you

I appreciate who you are and who you are becoming

I need you and your special gifts and talents

My thoughts, prayers, or affirmations

_____

_____

_____

_____

_____

_____

_____

_____

_____

_____

_____

_____

_____

It is perfectly
OKAY
TO BE
imperfect
and to make
MISTAKES

Life-Affirmations

About this spiritual tip: We sometimes pick up subtle or overt messages from our family of origin or from society which are untrue, shaming, or deny our humanity. Spoken or implied messages such as "you shouldn't feel angry" or "it's not okay to make mistakes" make it unnecessarily hard to be a human being. Even if we know intellectually that these messages are not true, they can still sneak up on us occasionally and negatively impact us with their lies.

Life-affirmations can help us to replace hurtful or crippling messages with healing and liberating ones. They can help counteract and defuse the power of any hurtful and untrue messages we may have picked up along the way. The ancient Hebrew people knew God as a freedom fighter, and we, too, can experience God's desire to help us break free from bondage to these harmful messages, so that we might live more peacefully and joyfully.

Applying and Activating

◆ Silently or aloud, slowly and prayerfully, read the list of affirmations two or more times.

15

- Spend time with the one affirmation you need most right now.
- Add some additional life-affirmations on the lines provided.
- Write down the most hurtful or unhelpful messages you have received about life and focus on the one or two that surface most frequently. Share these in prayer with God.

Life-Affirmations

It is perfectly okay to be imperfect and to make mistakes

Mistakes are not bad; they are simply opportunities for me to learn how to do things differently

Because I am a human being, I will experience a wide variety of emotions including anger, sadness, loneliness, and jealousy

It is normal to feel weak, vulnerable, and fragile at times

Everyone—not just me—makes poor choices in life and has regrets

It is healing to grieve and cry over the hurts I have suffered

The strength is within me to survive life's most painful moments

It is a sign of courage and strength to feel and face my fears

It is normal to feel powerless over many situations in my life

My thoughts, prayers, or affirmations

_____

_____

_____

_____

_____

_____

_____

_____

_____

_____

_____

_____

God is with me

God is with me

God is with me

God is with me

GOD IS
WITH ME

The Calming Balm of Mantras

About this spiritual tip: Children know how soothing repetition can be. They often love to hear the same stories, sing the same songs, and recite the same nursery rhymes again and again. An adult way to rediscover the calming effect repetition can have on our spirits is through the use of mantra prayers. A mantra is a short prayer phrase, usually eight syllables or less, which is repeated over and over, silently or aloud, in conjunction with our breath.

Mantras can be used in almost limitless ways: to help you slow down for prayer; as a way to focus your restless mind in prayer; to remind yourself of God's presence; or as an aid to help you through a challenging time, to name just a few possibilities. By spending just a short time with a mantra, you will often find it rising to your lips, peacefully penetrating your heart, and calming your mind throughout the day.

Applying and Activating

◆ Choose one of the following mantra prayers or create your own and repeat it over and over.

◆ Pray part of it as you inhale and part of it as you exhale.

- With each repetition, imagine yourself descending a set of stairs step by step to the very center of your being where God awaits you.
- Pray a mantra before or during a stressful meeting, a doctor or dentist appointment, or when resolving a conflict.

Mantras

Inhale	Exhale
God is	with me
Gentle God	comfort me
Spirit of God	help me
Creator God	guide me
Loving God	I need you
Comforting God	quiet my fears
God is near	God is here
God of peace	calm me
Indwelling God	strengthen me
Compassionate God	be with me

My thoughts, prayers, or affirmations

_____

_____

_____

_____

_____

_____

_____

_____

_____

_____

_____

Come to me,
all you that are
Weary
and
are carrying
heavy burdens,
and I will give you
REST.

MATTHEW 11:28

Seven Soothing Bible Verses

About this spiritual tip: During those times in life when we are feeling stressed or sad, fragile or fragmented, we can turn to the Bible and open ourselves to God's mothering comfort. We can pray with a consoling passage or verse which reminds us that underneath it all God is always there holding and supporting us.

Even if you are very strong and independent, it is okay to reach out and accept God's comforting and helping hand during life's stormy moments. When we do let God shoulder a portion of life's burdens, we, paradoxically, become more, rather than less, free. Our reliance upon the Creator strengthens and fosters our creative ability to cope with life's difficulties. Spending time with God's Word is a way to recall that we are never alone and that a Power greater than ourselves is always near to smooth and soothe the rough edges of our most stressful days.

Applying and Activating

- Slowly and prayerfully read through all seven verses once or twice, aloud if possible, pausing for ten or fifteen seconds between each verse.
- Read and pray one verse several times, as you turn your

concerns and difficulties over to the care of our loving God.

◆ Commit one verse to memory and carry it with you—
and allow it to carry you—throughout the day.

◆ Pray with other Bible verses that will help you experience
God's comforting presence.

Seven Soothing Bible Verses

Matthew 11:28 Come to me, all you that are weary and are
carrying heavy burdens, and I will give you rest.

Isaiah 43:1 Do not fear, for I have redeemed you; I have called
you by name, you are mine.

Psalm 18:2 The Lord is my rock, my fortress, my deliverer, my
God in whom I take refuge.

1 John 3:20 ...Whenever our hearts condemn us...God is
greater than our hearts....

Psalm 131:2 I have calmed and quieted my soul, like a weaned
child with its mother...

Genesis 28:15 Know that I am with you and will keep you
wherever you go...

Isaiah 43:4 You are precious in my sight, and honored, and I
love you.

My thoughts, prayers, or affirmations

_____

_____

_____

_____

_____

_____

_____

_____

_____

_____

_____

_____

Re(dis)covering Rest

About this spiritual tip: The incessant demands made on our time and energy wear us down, yet we often believe that getting more rest is simply not possible. But the truth is we can little afford not to take the time to get the physical and spiritual rest we need. Rest is a need—not an optional "want." And if our need for rest goes unmet, we suffer in subtle and not-so-subtle ways: stressed relationships, postponed or lost prayer life, poor or reactive choices, decreased effectiveness at work, loss of health, and so on. It is more difficult for many high achievers to stop their activities and rest for a while than it is to take on more projects and responsibilities and continue to do, do, do. Like toddlers who resist their naps—though they need them—we sometimes resist our need for rest. We can, however, rediscover the lost art of resting and relearn how to relax and be and "do" nothing. Our God of love calls us to honor our basic human need for rest. We must choose to respond to God's invitation.

Applying and Activating

- Write down all that needs doing and prioritize your list.
- Consider asking for help with those things that can be done by or with someone else.
- Make a plan for when you will "do" nothing but rest and relax.

+ Re-treat yourself with a good book, music, a movie, or something else that you enjoy.
+ Try the rest-inducing "activity" below.

Letting It All Go and Resting Peacefully in God's Love

Step One: Lie down on your bed with a pillow under your head and one or more pillows under your knees, so that your lower back is flat against the mattress.

Step Two: Rest your arms by your sides or place your interlaced fingers on your chest or stomach.

Step Three: Breathe slowly and deeply—your stomach should rise slightly as you inhale (more so than your chest) and return to its normal position as you exhale.

Step Four: Prayerfully repeat a mantra (God, I need your peace), an affirmation (I let go and rest in God's love), a Bible verse (Come to me and rest [Matthew 11:28]), or a single word (peace) to help you resist *do*-ing and to assist you in *be*-ing.

Step Five: Imagine God supporting you like your bed, and with each breath and repetition of your mantra, Bible verse, affirmation, or word let all your worries, responsibilities, and fatigue drop into God's care.

My thoughts, prayers, or affirmations

_____

_____

_____

_____

_____

_____

_____

_____

_____

_____

_____

_____

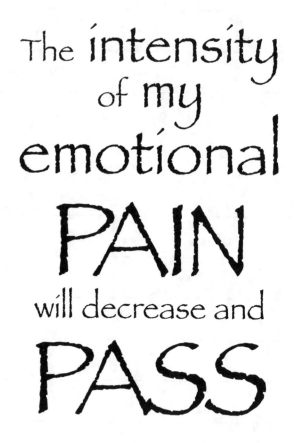

The intensity of my emotional PAIN will decrease and PASS

Praying Painful Emotions

About this spiritual tip: Painful feelings can be difficult to accept and express in healthy ways. Many times we find ourselves resisting or suppressing feelings such as fear or anger. While the ideal is to embrace our painful feelings, more realistic goals might be to accept them as part of being a human being and to flow with their comings and goings.

Painful emotions often act as messengers. Loneliness, sadness, shame, guilt, anger, fear, inadequacy…can inform us of when and where we might be out of balance, of what we need, and of the call to exercise self-care. For example, when I feel shame after I have acted poorly in a particular situation, it is letting me know that I need to nurture, affirm, and be gentle with myself. Feelings of shame remind me to separate my behavior—which is sometimes good and sometimes not—from my unchangeable goodness as a person. We can learn to turn toward, rather than away, from God when we are suffering emotional pain and allow God to heal us. Divine help is always just a prayer away.

Applying and Activating

- Name what you are feeling as precisely as possible and what thoughts, events, or memories have contributed to your feeling.
- Be with the pain by saying something like, "I feel (name the emotion) right now. I don't like this feeling, but I choose to just let it pass through me."
- Decrease the intensity of your emotional pain by talking about it with another person.
- Recall how you have survived these feelings in the past as evidence that you will survive them again.
- Refer to some of the other spiritual tips.
- Allow one of the following affirmations or truths to serve as a doorway to prayer.

Affirmations and Truths for Coping with Emotional Pain

The intensity of my emotional pain will gradually decrease and pass

Although I am hurting, I know that I am not alone

This feeling does not define me; I am more than my feelings

I listen for the messages my painful feelings may have for me and consider what actions I might take

I delay making any important decisions until I regain my emotional equilibrium

Because I am important to others, I choose to reach out and seek the support of my community

It is okay to feel exactly what I am feeling at this moment

My thoughts, prayers, or affirmations

_____

_____

_____

_____

_____

_____

_____

_____

_____

_____

_____

I am grateful
for the gifts
and blessings
I have received

Expressing Gratitude

About this spiritual tip: A sure sign of spiritual growth is a sense of gratefulness for the blessings we have received from our generous God. While gratitude cannot be forced, it can be cultivated. It is not just a feeling that comes and goes like our other emotions; rather, it is an attitude that recognizes and receives every good thing in our lives—some of which are born from life's not-so-good experiences—as pure gift.

A grateful person realizes that such basics as health, food, water, and shelter are incredible gifts that are often taken for granted. A grateful person appreciates new opportunities, life's abundant second chances, renewed meaning and purpose, satisfying work, and intimate relationships. The Great Gift Giver is eager to lavish goodness upon us. The stance we need to strive for is one of openness and gratitude.

Applying and Activating

- To get in the gratitude habit, thank God for two or three blessings each day.
- Thank God for those blessings and gifts that you often take for granted, such as having a bed to sleep on.

- Review the past week and express gratitude for your positive and growthful experiences.
- Thank God for the personal gifts you have developed as a result of the pain you have suffered in life (compassion, for example).
- Express gratitude for some of the unexpected and surprising blessings you have received.

Three Gratitude Exercises

1. Wherever you are at this moment, look around at your surroundings very carefully, as if you are looking through the lens of a video camera. Looking at your environment with eyes of gratitude, spend some time thanking God for what you see.

2. Call to mind significant people who have had a positive and healing impact on you. Name some of the blessings you have received from each of them.

3. At different times if you only have a few minutes, or at one sitting if you have a bigger block of time, write down the five or ten most significant blessings you have received during each of these periods of your life: childhood, teen years, twenties, thirties, and each subsequent five- or ten-year period up to your current age.

My thoughts, prayers, or affirmations

_____

_____

_____

_____

_____

_____

_____

_____

_____

_____

_____

_____

I TRUST in

God's loving

and active presence

in the lives of those for

whom I PRAY

Praying for Others

About this spiritual tip: Stepping outside and beyond ourselves is an essential component of spiritual and psychological health. Setting aside our own problems and agenda to focus on someone else reminds us that everyone has their difficulties and tough moments in life. Praying for others is beneficial for them and for us. We sense our interconnectedness, mutual fragility, and amazing resilience. We come to a greater recognition of our need for each other's compassion and empathy and of our dependence upon God. God's love flows most powerfully through the care and prayer we extend to each other. When we pray for others, our trust in God's loving presence and active involvement in their lives is strengthened, however imperceptibly. We are reassured that neither they nor we are alone. God is with us all!

Applying and Activating

- Focus on one person who needs God's loving presence, such as a family member, coworker, or stranger.
- Consider turning your prayer into action by reaching out to this person.
- Identify and pray for someone whom you dislike or look down on.

- Pray for a group of people you would just as soon dismiss—members of another religion, sexual orientation, political viewpoint, or philosophy.
- Pray for someone who is no longer in your life. It might be a childhood friend, a teacher, or a former neighbor or boss.

One Way to Pray for Another

Step One: Identify one person for whom you would like to pray and take a couple of moments to ponder what he or she thinks, feels, fears, hopes, suffers, wants, or needs.

Step Two: Call to mind that God is with you as you express your concern.

Step Three: Imagine God's healing love and your love descending upon, surrounding, or penetrating this person and repeat several times: "God is loving (Name) as I pray."

Step Four: Tell God what you think he or she needs such as healing, a new job, guidance, or hope.

Step Five: Close with something like the following: "Loving God, you see (Name) more clearly than I do, and I trust you to continue to be with him/her. I believe you will always provide for (Name), and I pray that he/she will somehow be able to sense your active and compassionate presence in his/her life. I trust in your love for (Name)."

My thoughts, prayers, or affirmations

_____

_____

_____

_____

_____

_____

_____

_____

_____

_____

_____

_____

God is near,

God is
here

Recalling God's Nearness

About this spiritual tip: Our heart beats continuously, but we are usually unaware of it unless we are exerting ourselves physically. In the same way, God is with us and is supporting us at every moment, but we often have little or no sense of God's presence in our lives. One way to become more aware of our heart is to engage in some type of aerobic exercise. One way to become more aware of God's heartfelt presence in our lives is to turn our attention toward God. We can do this by committing some time—perhaps ten or twenty minutes—to daily prayer and meditation. We can also become more aware of God's presence by just pausing periodically during the day to recall and affirm that God is near, that God is here. We can remember that God is with us in peaceful and joyous moments—a beautiful sunrise or sunset, a sense of inner contentment, satisfaction in the completion of a project—and in the stressful and painful moments of life—a loss, a conflict, or a moment of failure.

Applying and Activating

- Slowly and prayerfully repeat several times a prayer affirmation such as "God is near" or "God is with me."
- Visualize the light of God shining on you, arising in you, or surrounding you like a protective shield and bask in the warmth of this supportive and healing light.
- Imagine God at your side as you face a challenging situation, such as a rapidly approaching deadline or an important meeting.
- Recall a time when you felt God to be especially near and allow this memory to fill you with a sense of how near God is to you at this moment.
- Use a tangible aid, such as the lighting of a candle or setting an empty chair across from the one you are sitting on to represent God's unseen—but very real—presence.
- Pray with one or more of the following affirmations.

Affirmations for Recalling God's Nearness

God is near, God is here

God is with me as I (name the situation you are facing)

I breathe in God's presence and breathe out my sense of aloneness

God is with me and is supporting me at each and every moment of my life

In good times and bad, God is here

My thoughts, prayers, or affirmations

_____

_____

_____

_____

_____

_____

_____

_____

_____

_____

_____

_____

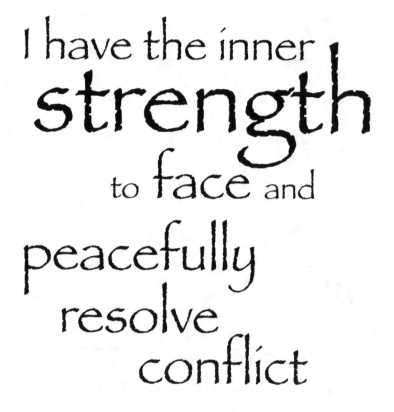

I have the inner strength to face and peacefully resolve conflict

Coping with Conflict

About this spiritual tip: Many of us either hate or fear conflict. Conflict can be especially upsetting when we are having a perfectly peaceful day, and it suddenly appears out of the blue. An unexpected caustic remark at work sends us reeling or a discussion at home turns heated and hurtful words are hurled. When we experience conflict, our thinking often becomes distorted and muddled. Our heart rate tends to increase and our breathing becomes more shallow, as we prepare to "fight or take flight." Inner peace instantly disappears as anxiety and tension barge in. While most of us do not seek conflict, it is part of life, it is part of being an imperfect person who lives with, works with, and simply shares this planet with other imperfect people. The good news is that we are not totally powerless, because we have an Expert in conflict resolution who is eager to help us reclaim our personal power, as we take the initial steps toward resolving conflict in peaceful and respectful ways.

Applying and Activating

◆ Ask God for the grace to say nothing until you have calmed down, especially if you sense that destructive and reactionary words are on the tip of your tongue.

- Ask God for divine ideas to help resolve or partially resolve the conflict.
- When the other person does not want to take the high road, ask God for the strength to walk it alone.
- Be extra gentle and self-nurturing, especially if you were more reactive than proactive during a moment of conflict.
- Refer to some of the other spiritual tips to help you regain your balance, perhaps # 1, 4, 5, 7, or 10.
- Read and pray with the following affirmations.

Affirmations and Truths for Coping with Conflict

While I don't like conflict, I am strong enough to survive its comings and goings

Conflict is a healthy aspect of life when it is faced with courage and creativity

I am getting better at handling and resolving conflict; I don't have to be perfect

When I blow it, I will apologize and make amends—if it is safe to do so

God loves me even when, in my humanity, I yearn to return hurt for hurt

While revenge might be temporarily satisfying, I will feel even worse if I act on it

God is with me during this difficult moment and is holding me in protective love

My thoughts, prayers, or affirmations

_____

_____

_____

_____

_____

_____

_____

_____

_____

_____

_____

_____

_____

_____

As I
own my fears,
my fears
no longer
own me

Facing Fear

About this spiritual tip: Fear, perhaps more than any other emotion, is one we resist and push away. Because fear is so uncomfortable, we may try to distract ourselves in countless ways. I have even tried to "pray it away," which usually doesn't work until I face it, feel it, and listen to what it is telling me.

Our childhood fears have left an indelible imprint upon our psyches and are often reactivated when we encounter our fears today. Childhood fears amplify our adult fears, unless we offer our frightened inner child—and inner adult—the reassurances we may not have received in childhood. We can use our minds to remind ourselves that fear is only an emotion, and that it does not run our lives. Fear simply needs to be felt and listened to as it flows through us. If we run, and often that is our first response, the power of fear only grows larger, like our shadows on a sunny summer evening. We can choose to stop running and turn to God for comfort and support as we face, feel, own, and befriend our fears.

Applying and Activating

◆ Rather than push your fear away, stay with it and pray, "God is with me as I feel this fear."

- When your mind races from one fearful thought to another, slow it down by writing your fears on paper.
- Pray for the courage to take the next necessary—and brave—step toward facing your fear, rather than trying to conquer it all at once.
- Remember that your healthy fears are friends who only want to keep you safe.
- Confront your unhealthy fears when they bully you and try to keep you from taking necessary risks.
- Spend some time reflecting upon the following affirmations and truths.

Affirmations and Truths for Facing Fear

As an adult, I have the inner courage and strength to face and feel this fear

I listen to fear and then discern what choices or changes I need to make

It is healthy and healing to share my fears with another person

When I see fear as a friend rather than as a foe, it is much more likely to flow

My fears, like all my other emotions, will become less intense as I face them

As I own my fears, my fears will no longer own me

God is with me, encouraging me to be strong and courageous

My thoughts, prayers, or affirmations

_____

_____

_____

_____

_____

_____

_____

_____

_____

_____

_____

_____

_____

GOD and I
are PARTNERS,
and TOGETHER
we have
a DYNAMIC,
interdependent
RELATIONSHIP

The Partnership of Prayer

About this spiritual tip: When we were children, many of our prayers were, in effect, wishes. God was to act like a fairy or genie and fix what was broken or supply what was missing. Despite our most passionate prayers, significant hurts were not always healed and crucial needs were not always met. Childlike trust, innocence, and naivete gradually moved out, and disappointment and distrust moved in. While innocence and naivete are forever gone and have nothing to offer us as adults, we can rebuild our trust in God by growing in our understanding of how prayer "works" and what it requires of us.

An adult stance—or dance—is one in which we approach prayer as a dynamic partnership. The word "dynamic" is defined as "vigorously active and energetic," which describes the interdependent roles both God and we have to play in prayer. Prayer is a relationship of mutual responsibility and responsiveness. We don't pray and then sit back; rather, we pray and act. Our human efforts join with the Divine in prayer and in response to prayer.

Applying and Activating

- Tell God what you need from the partnership and ask what God needs from you.
- Identify a problem with which you would like God's help and discern what action you can take, as well as how God can help you.
- Affirm regularly that God is actively and intimately involved in your life.
- Look back and recall how God has helped you in specific situations, even though you may not have felt God's presence at the time.
- Reflect upon or pray with the following affirmations and truths.

Affirmations and Truths about the Dynamic Partnership of Prayer

God and I are partners, and together we have a dynamic, interdependent partnership

I do what I can and trust God to take care of that which is beyond my personal power

Even when I don't know *how* God is involved, I trust that God *is* intimately involved

When I let God help me, I rediscover the God-given power I have to help myself

I need God's energy and love; God needs my effort and love

In some situations, God will count on me to carry the larger portion of the load

In some situations, I will count on God to carry the larger portion of the load

My thoughts, prayers, or affirmations

_____

_____

_____

_____

_____

_____

_____

_____

_____

_____

_____

_____

_____

_____

I totally
accept God's
forgiveness
as well as
my own

Accepting Forgiveness

About this spiritual tip: For a variety of reasons, some of us seem unable to experience God's forgiveness and to fully forgive ourselves. Some say we are being arrogant when we don't forgive ourselves, even though God has forgiven us. But maybe arrogance isn't the problem. Even though we intellectually believe in a forgiving God, perhaps we haven't experienced God's forgiveness. Experience has to support our theological beliefs or they are rendered meaningless. God's forgiveness is also elusive if we are reluctant to forgive ourselves, for both are intimately linked. Like twins who are physically joined together at birth, one can't go or grow anywhere without the other.

Engaging in some type of ceremony can help us experience both God's forgiveness as well as our own. Ancient peoples knew the power of ceremonies in helping them overcome the mysterious dark forces surrounding them. Our inability to forgive ourselves and to know God's forgiveness experientially is a dark force we can take steps to overcome. The light of forgiveness does shine in the darkness and gently beckons us.

Applying and Activating

+ Determine if you have perceptions of God as a harsh or punishing judge, and if so, begin to replace these with gentler images and understandings.

+ Write down events for which you struggle to forgive yourself and ceremonially bury the paper in a garden or burn it as a way of letting the past go.

+ See your failings in behavioral terms by praying the following: "Forgiving God, help me to completely forgive myself and to accept your total forgiveness for (name the behavior)."

+ For each memory of when you hurt someone, recall a time when you helped someone.

+ Create and read forgiveness affirmations.

+ Share your forgiveness struggles with a spiritual advisor or friend.

A Forgiveness Ceremony

Step One: Gaze compassionately upon a baby or childhood picture of yourself.

Step Two: See how fragile, dependent, and in need of nurturing you were at that age.

Step Three: Gaze at a current picture of yourself with the same eyes of compassion.

Step Four: Imagine God gazing at you with complete compassion and total forgiveness.

Step Five: Embrace both pictures next to your heart and accept God's embrace.

My thoughts, prayers, or affirmations

_____

_____

_____

_____

_____

_____

_____

_____

_____

_____

_____

_____

_____

To resent
is human...

To resent AGAIN
is more human...

To resent YET AGAIN
is most human

Reducing Resilient Resentments

About this spiritual tip: We human beings are tremendously resilient, as we are able to bounce back from all sorts of setbacks and losses in life. One aspect of our humanity that we sometimes wish wasn't so resilient is our proclivity to feel resentful toward those people or institutions that have hurt us. Despite our best efforts to forgive and move on, resentments tend to resurface again and again. It's almost as if they have a life of their own and don't want us to ever forgive our offenders!

Resentments re-send to our conscious awareness specific memories of how we have been hurt in the recent or distant past. We may feel intense hatred as we fantasize disturbing scenes of retribution. And then shame or guilt may torment us for even having such thoughts and feelings—especially if we are trying to live as spiritual people. But resentments, like all feelings, simply have a message for us. They tell us we have suffered an injustice and have been hurt. They remind us that we need the healing touch of the Divine Healer and of our call to serve as co-healers by being extraordinarily gentle with and accepting of ourselves.

Applying and Activating

- Ask God for the grace to stay with and befriend the feelings of resentment rather than suppress them.
- Speak aloud or write down your resentful feelings: "I resent (name or institution) for (hurt inflicted)."
- Share your feelings with God or another person.
- Discern if some current stress or hurt has triggered old, painful memories.
- Prayerfully read the following affirmations and truths.

Affirmations and Truths to Help Reduce Resilient Resentments

It is perfectly normal and human to feel resentful toward someone who has hurt me

By befriending and giving voice to my resentment, I reduce its power over me

Like all emotions, the intensity of this feeling of resentment will decrease and pass

I completely accept myself when I have resentful feelings and vindictive urges

I choose to be gentle with myself as I re-suffer the pain of this resentment

God totally accepts me and desires to help me through the pain of this resentment

To resent is human, to resent again is more human, to resent yet again is most human

My thoughts, prayers, or affirmations

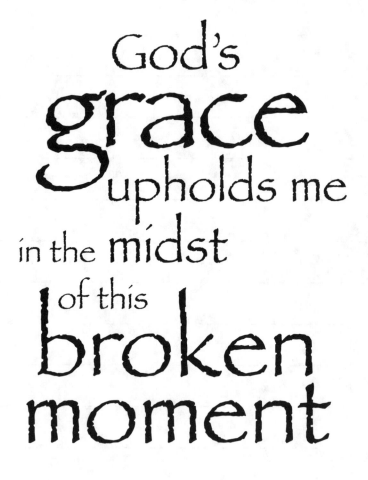

God's
grace
upholds me
in the midst
of this
broken
moment

Grace in Broken Moments

About this spiritual tip: Despite our best efforts to act in concert with our values and spirituality, we all suffer broken and grace-less moments. Fortunately, our worst behavior is usually witnessed by only a few people—often in the privacy of our homes. Sometimes no one knows how poorly we acted and, as a result, we risk sinking into silent and isolating shame: "If only she, he, they knew what I did!"

As flawed individuals, we are prone to making mistakes, to reacting in conflicts, and to quite simply and painfully blowing it at times. God's love and acceptance, however, are not based upon our behavior. Brought into existence out of God's great love, we are loved simply because we exist. There are no performance clauses attached to God's passionate and constant love, for we are loved when we are at our best *and* when we are at our worst. As we open up to God's grace-filled unconditional love, we receive the necessary grace and self-acceptance to bounce back more quickly from our inevitable broken moments in life.

Applying and Activating

◆ Share your broken moment with someone you trust so that

you don't sink into the quagmire of shame.

- Offer the reassuring and supportive words to yourself (aloud if possible) that you would say to a friend if he or she were facing a similar situation.
- Ask God to help you focus on your behavior, rather than condemn yourself as a person, by saying aloud: "I forgive myself for (behavior)."
- Refer to some of the other spiritual tips.
- Soak in the affirmations and truths below.

Affirmations and Truths for Coping with Broken Moments

In my grace-less moments, I open up to God's grace-filled love and acceptance

God's comforting and tender love upholds me in the midst of this broken moment

Because I am an imperfect person, I will not handle each and every situation perfectly

I choose to learn from the pain of this broken moment, make amends, and try again

Everybody—not just me—speaks or acts poorly at times, so I am not alone or unique

As I accept God's acceptance and forgiveness, I am able to accept and forgive myself

This broken moment does not define me nor does it negate the many things I do well

To help regain my perspective, I choose to remember some of my best moments

My thoughts, prayers, or affirmations

_____

_____

_____

_____

_____

_____

_____

_____

_____

_____

_____

_____

When I feel
like I am
falling apart,
I trust
that I will
be caught

Caught Falling Apart

About this spiritual tip: The struggles and stresses of modern living combined with life's inevitable heartaches and losses weigh us down. We can reach a point when life—even the ordinary stuff of life—seems extraordinarily heavy and difficult. It is not uncommon to feel anxious, depressed, or overwhelmed by it all. Whatever the factors—the daily grind, personal problems, or the desire to make a little sense out of life—we long to be able to call a "time-out" in a world that never stops.

Perhaps on the outside very few are aware of what is largely an inner struggle. Needing to maintain our public images and perform well at work, we respond with insincere smiles and the expected "fine" or "good" when asked how we are, while inside we may feel like we're falling apart. Blinking back tears or actually breaking down in tears may be happening more often. The churning in our gut or the tight feeling in our chest tell us we're at a breaking point. While we don't want to crumble in front of our coworkers or casual acquaintances, we *can* fall apart and trust we will be caught by the Tender One who knows and understands all that is really going on deep within us. We can also try to treat ourselves tenderly as well.

Applying and Activating

- Allow yourself to fall apart and benefit from a cleansing cry.
- Tell God or a friend, in no uncertain terms, that you can't take it anymore!
- Write down all that is weighing heavily upon you.
- Place your list of burdens next to your chest and just be with the heaviness for a while.
- Identify what is most heavy or troubling and ask for God's help.
- Pray for divine ideas on how you and God can lighten your load.
- Put on some peaceful music and read the following affirmations and truths.

Affirmations and Truths about Falling Apart

God is with me and is holding me during this painful moment

In my weakness and vulnerability, God is my Strength and constant Support

I will share what is really going on inside me with someone I trust

When I feel like I'm falling apart, I trust that I will be caught

I choose to make some healthy choices to help myself through this difficult time

One by one, I release my troubles, burdens, and responsibilities into God's tender care

My thoughts, prayers, or affirmations

_____

_____

_____

_____

_____

_____

_____

_____

_____

_____

_____

_____

_____

I choose to
befriend
my anger
and to be
befriended
by my anger

Befriending Anger

About this spiritual tip: Neglected and rejected anger is like the school bully whose own hurts cause him to hurt others. Children quickly learn to avoid the bully as much as possible, so as not to become victims of his unpredictable abuse. Occasionally a brave soul stands up to him, and in the process, a mutual friendship begins. The bully's need for a friend helps heal his desire to lash out and hurt others.

So it is with anger. When we treat our anger as a friend and listen to its messages, we will be less prone to lashing out and hurting others in wild, unpredictable ways. As a friend, anger wants us to acknowledge and deal with our hurts, which roam a continuum ranging from minor disappointments to slanderous attacks to an unexpected and devastating betrayal. Anger is a friend who is filled with energy and very much needs our friendship and guidance so that its energy can be released in healthy and constructive ways. Learning how to express our anger energy in healthy ways is a two-steps-forward-one-step-backward process. Blowing it, regression, often precedes our next growth spurt, progression. Fortunately, we have a God who will always befriend us—and our anger—during each step of the process.

Applying and Activating

◆ Speak aloud your feelings of anger: "I feel angry at (who or what) because (tell why)."

◆ Stay with your anger, befriend it, and release it by engaging in some physical activity.

◆ Thank your anger for its friendship and for how it wants you to acknowledge and deal with your hurts and frustrations.

◆ When your anger energy has been released somewhat, risk confronting the other person.

◆ If it is not safe to talk to the person or if he or she refuses or is unable to be accountable, seek out the support of a friend.

Affirmations and Truths for Befriending Anger

I choose to befriend my anger and to be befriended by my anger

I claim my anger as a lifelong friend, who only wants to help me deal with my hurts

When I express my anger in positive ways, I will celebrate the progress I am making

When I express my anger poorly, I will make amends, forgive myself, and try again

It is okay to feel angry toward those who have hurt me and refuse to be accountable

I will feel and deal with my anger *before* I make any efforts to forgive

My thoughts, prayers, or affirmations

I believe
wholeheartedly
that GOD
desires my
greatest
GOOD
and is worthy
of my TRUST

Toward Deeper Trust

About this spiritual tip: Sometimes we mistakenly think that trust is just a feeling over which we have very little control. We either have trust or we don't and there's not much we can do about it. But trust is also an attitude, an approach to life which can be nurtured and developed. Of course there are all sorts of valid reasons why it can be hard to trust God and other people, such as hurtful childhood experiences, rigid religious training, broken relationships, and the various losses that accumulate over the years. But these trust-busters can become the very foundation upon which a deeper sense of trust is rebuilt, for spiritual teachers tell us that our deepest wounds are often the source of our deepest healing.

The God-given gift of trust is within each of us, waiting to be uncovered and recovered. Like someone who is fearful of water, we begin by sitting at the shallow end of the pool and cautiously dangling our feet in the water. At our own pace, we gently ease into the water, and in the process, our fears and wounds begin to heal. Over time and incrementally, we move toward the deeper water and discover that God, like the water, supports us and is worthy of our deepest trust.

Applying and Activating

- Allow the voice of distrust to speak its fears and to be acknowledged by you.
- Allow the inner voice of trust to gently comfort the voice of distrust, perhaps in a written dialogue.
- Share your fears and worries with someone you trust.
- Ask God to help you reclaim your God-given ability to trust.
- Write down what your life would be like with more trust and keep this vision before you.
- Read the following affirmations and truths regularly to help nurture trust's growth within you.

Affirmations and Truths for Deeper Trust

I believe that I can gradually and over time become a person of deep trust

I believe wholeheartedly that God desires my greatest good and is worthy of my trust

I choose to practice trust by reaching out to the supportive people in my life

With trust, I place my struggles, my fears, and my very life into God's care

I trust myself to make healthy choices and to take the necessary risks to live happily

With Julian of Norwich, I repeat over and over, "all shall be well, all shall be well…"

My thoughts, prayers, or affirmations

I choose to accept God's gift of unconditional love

Accepting Unconditional Love

About this spiritual tip: Perhaps some of us have wondered if our friends and family would still love us if conditions changed. If we became seriously ill, developed a drinking problem, were disabled, got fired, suffered depression, or lost our faith… would we still be loved? We hope the answer would be yes. Yet we sometimes wonder what the limits of human love are.

Deep inside we long to be loved unconditionally as we were during our infancy. We fear the loss of love because as we grew older, conditions were attached to what was once freely and unconditionally given: *if* we did what the teachers wanted, we were praised; *if* we achieved what our parents wanted for us, we received their approval; *if* we met the requirements established by our peers, we were accepted. And now as adults, meeting conditions continues to play a big part in getting what we need and want, whether it is at our work or in our relationships. No wonder it is so hard to believe that God loves and accepts us unconditionally! No wonder it is so hard to love and accept ourselves unconditionally! But we can (re)turn to the God who loves us without condition and (re)learn to accept God's gift of unconditional love.

Applying and Activating

◆ Offer words of unconditional love to yourself by repeating, "I love myself completely and unconditionally."

◆ Allow God to speak words of unconditional love, "You are loved completely and unconditionally."

◆ Name some conditional messages you have picked up such as, "I am lovable only if I lose twenty pounds," and replace it with unconditional messages, "I am lovable just the way I am!"

An Exercise in Accepting Unconditional Love

Accepting unconditional love is often most difficult when we are keenly cognizant of our mistakes and shortcomings, yet our need for unconditional love is never greater than when we have lost self-perspective, so we pray and affirm:

"The conditioned adult in me, because of years of practice, feels compelled to reject myself and to refuse God's love and my own love because (name the shortcoming, failure, thoughts, or feelings), but led by the infant within and with the grace of God, I completely accept myself and accept God's complete and unconditional love for me *as* I am."

My thoughts, prayers, or affirmations

_____

_____

_____

_____

_____

_____

_____

_____

_____

_____

_____

_____

_____

God desires
  to help me move from
    the PAIN
of bitterness
    to the PEACE
of better~ness

From Bitterness
to Better-ness

About this spiritual tip: Our emotional and spiritual wounds have the potential to make us better people or bitter people. And although the healing process may take many years, there comes a time when we stand at the crossroads and must choose between getting better or remaining bitter. Perhaps this moment of decision arises after we have done some significant work in therapy or have been involved in a Twelve-Step program or some other kind of support group, but we know deep inside that the choice is now ours and ours alone. We realize that life will continue to pass us by and unhappiness will be our closest companion unless we take *full* responsibility for our life's direction.

Feeling bitter is certainly understandable, especially considering how deeply the hurts of childhood, adolescence, and our adult years run. But the price of remaining bitter is extremely high: lost opportunities, unhappiness, feeling disconnected from God and others, dissatisfying relationships, and so on. We need to leave our pain behind us, for it has been said that even God cannot change the past. God, who knows the depths of our bitterness, desires that we know a better future. God wants us to choose life to the full.

Applying and Activating

- Name the person(s) or events you feel bitter about and rate the intensity of your bitterness on a scale of one to ten.
- Ask God to be with you in the midst of your bitterness.
- Consider writing down the payoffs for remaining bitter and the payoffs for getting better.
- Identify what you can do to facilitate your healing, such as therapy, joining a support group, or spending time in prayer.
- If a tunnel of one hundred yards symbolized the passage from bitterness to better-ness, how far along are you and how can you continue to move toward the light?
- Dream of what a bitter-less and better future would be like.

An Exercise to Help Move from Bitterness to Better-ness

Step One: Name your deepest bitterness (a former spouse, boss, coworker, or illness...).

Step Two: Write a letter to God—or to the person—pouring out the depth of your pain and anger.

Step Three: Consider sharing your letter with a spiritual advisor or friend.

Step Four: Ceremonially burn, bury, or rip up the letter as a way of letting the past go.

Step Five: Consider buying or creating something for yourself to help celebrate a new beginning.

My thoughts, prayers, or affirmations

_____

_____

_____

_____

_____

_____

_____

_____

_____

_____

_____

_____

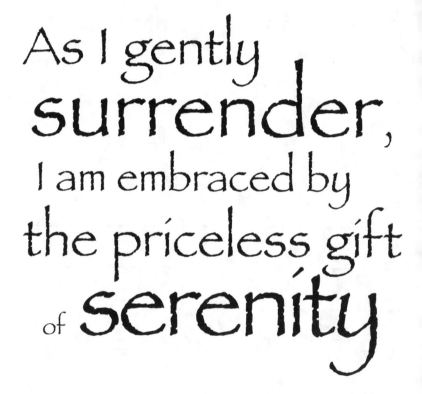

As I gently surrender, I am embraced by the priceless gift of serenity

The Serenity of Surrendering

About this spiritual tip: Hard work, perseverance, and going the extra mile are traits that contribute greatly to our ability to succeed. One characteristic not usually associated with success, however, is that of surrender. A time comes when hard work, etc., gets us no further than flooring the gas pedal will when our car is stuck in snow. Only by taking our foot off the gas pedal, only by lightening up and surrendering, can we hope to discover a creative solution. Those who learn to surrender, to concede, to yield, to relinquish the struggle, are the ones who live serenely. Paradoxically, when we learn to surrender, we are as effective—maybe even more so—in our personal and professional lives as when we are driven, forceful, pushy, or controlling.

When our prayer life is a struggle, surrendering our efforts, rather than trying harder, brings us peace—and prayer. When we try to control someone, surrendering is the one-way road to regaining control of ourselves and to recovering our serenity. When we try to force an outcome, surrendering and accepting that we did our best helps us flow with whatever does or doesn't turn out. As we learn to surrender, we will end up surrendering our serenity less often.

Applying and Activating

◆ Determine if there are any situations or relationships you are trying to force or control and pay attention to how you are thinking and feeling.

◆ Try surrendering the situation or relationship and see if your thoughts and feelings become more serene.

◆ If it is difficult to surrender completely, consider what mini-steps you can take to partially surrender.

◆ Identify the payoffs for practicing the art of surrender and the payoffs for continuing to try to control.

◆ Reflect upon or pray with the following affirmations and truths.

Affirmations and Truths for Surrendering

I would rather surrender when it is wise to do so than surrender my serenity

As I gently yield and surrender, I am embraced by the priceless gift of serenity

When I revert to controlling, I will surrender to the fact that I am simply human

The serenity of surrendering far outweighs whatever can be gained from controlling

When something doesn't work out, surrendering frees me to try something different

When I surrender, I often discover new and surprising solutions to my problems

My thoughts, prayers, or affirmations

_____

_____

_____

_____

_____

_____

_____

_____

_____

_____

_____

_____

When I am out-of-balance,

I WILL take some
SIMPLE steps to
become more
BALANCED

Living a More Balanced Life

About this spiritual tip: During any given twenty-four hour day, many of us would rather spend more time doing X and less time doing Y. We might exercise more if our work commute was shorter and less tiring; we might read more if our children's needs were less incessant; we might devote more time to a hobby or interest if our weekends weren't so busy; we might pray more if meals and laundry and a dozen other daily chores took less time, and so on.

Despite all our time-saving technology, we seem to have less time to spend! Out-of-balance, we may feel powerless to regain our balance. How do we even begin?! As with most overwhelming problems, the solution usually begins with a simple first step. We begin small, perhaps by planning to exercise just one or two days each week, by reading during a work break rather than in the evening, by spending a couple of hours on our hobby or interest two weekends each month rather than every weekend, and by praying during our daily commute. We let go of the unattainable ideal and accept what is real: we have a limited amount of time and energy to spend each day. And as we make creative choices, we reclaim our personal power and regain our balance.

Applying and Activating

◆ Keep track of how you are spending your time for one week and discern what changes you need to make to live with more balance.

◆ Take advantage of short time periods, fifteen to thirty minutes, to do what is good for you.

◆ When you say something like, "I *have* to work long hours," rephrase it by saying, "I *choose* to work long hours."

◆ Envision what a more balanced life would entail and take a simple first step to help make it a reality.

◆ Reflect upon the following affirmations or truths.

For Living a More Balanced Life

This day, I choose to take full responsibility for how I spend my time and energy

As I reclaim my personal power of choice, my life becomes more balanced

When I am out-of-balance, I will take some simple steps to become more balanced

While there is much I *have* to do, there is also much I can *choose* to do—or not do

When I feel overwhelmed, I will recognize it as a sign that I may be out-of-balance

It is within my personal power to live a life that is well-balanced and satisfying

My thoughts, prayers, or affirmations

_____

_____

_____

_____

_____

_____

_____

_____

_____

_____

_____

_____

_____

I choose to
acknowledge
and
CELEBRATE
the progress
I am making

Celebrating Progress— Not Perfection

About this spiritual tip: Acknowledging and celebrating how we have grown and changed is something many of us rarely do, especially if we have perfectionist tendencies. Perhaps we have been making enormous progress in an area that has been historically difficult for us, anger, for example. But should we experience just one moment of failure, one return visit to some deeply ingrained behavior patterns, we tend to negate and discount all the improvement we have made! Our moment of failure leads us into the lonely land of lost perspective.

In one of Jesus' parables, he tells a story of the shepherd who left the ninety-nine sheep to go searching for the one lost sheep (Luke 15:1–7). We, however, must leave behind our one "bad" moment—of poorly expressed anger or whatever it might be— and go searching for the ninety-nine "good" moments, for the many times we have made progress in this challenging aspect of our lives. And then, we imitate the shepherd by celebrating what we have found, in this case, our perspective. As we acknowledge and celebrate our progress more often, perfectionism loses its power over us, perspective is regained, and personal power and peace return to us.

Applying and Activating

- Identify some areas that have been, or still are, difficult for you and write down some specific ways you have grown and made progress.
- Celebrate your progress with a friend, perhaps over a cup of gourmet coffee, or buy yourself a small gift.
- When perfectionism falsely accuses you of making no progress, seek perspective by journaling, talking with a friend, or praying.
- Rather than trying to rid yourself of perfectionism, thank it for inspiring you to do well but also discipline and restrain it when it gets carried away.
- Read and reflect upon the following affirmations and truths.

Affirmations and Truths for Overcoming Perfectionism

Whenever I fail, I will remember how I have succeeded in the past and try again

Perfection is not attainable, but progress, perspective, personal power, and peace are well within my reach

I choose to acknowledge and celebrate the progress I am making

When perfectionism sinks me, recalling how I have made progress saves me

My thoughts, prayers, or affirmations

_____

_____

_____

_____

_____

_____

_____

_____

_____

_____

_____

_____

_____

Within my weaknesses

lie some of
my potential
strengths

Turning Weaknesses in to Strengths

About this spiritual tip: Many of our personal gifts and strengths have evolved only because we have wrestled with our faults and weaknesses. Whatever our shortcomings might be, such as tendencies to criticize, judge, or worry, a potential gift lies hidden within each. Criticism can be transformed into praise; being judgmental can evolve into acceptance; worry can become trust, and so on.

The process of a weakness becoming a gift or strength is a slow one and involves both our efforts and God's grace. First, we need to name, own, and feel the pain our weaknesses cause us or others. If we are judgmental, we would say something like, "At times, I spend a lot of energy judging others and I feel sad about it." Then, we name the potential gift or strength hidden within, which is often the opposite of the weakness, and say, "I want to become more accepting of myself and others."

As we try to change and be changed, we remember that the process is not linear. We pray, progress and regress, and seek help or support. Gradually, the strength of our weakness weakens and the weakness of our strength strengthens. A gift we never imagined possible for us has now become something we can share with others!

Applying and Activating

- Identify some of your gifts which have arisen from wrestling with your weaknesses.
- Name one of your weaknesses or shortcomings and the painful effects it has on your life or on the lives of others.
- Name the opposite of this weakness or shortcoming and identify the positive benefits it could bring to your life or others.
- Remember that the journey from weakness to strength is one of single steps and discern what step you can take today.
- When you regress, forgive yourself, and expect to progress even further in the very near future.
- Read and reflect upon the following affirmations and truths.

Affirmations and Truths for Transforming Our Weaknesses

Within my weaknesses lie some of my potential strengths

I choose to work on my weaknesses so that they may, one day, become my strengths

I allow the pain my weaknesses and shortcomings cause me or others to become a catalyst for making positive changes

I believe that each step I take leads me closer to the gifts that lie hidden within my weaknesses

My weaknesses are parts of me that need my tender care and unconditional love

My thoughts, prayers, or affirmations

_____

_____

_____

_____

_____

_____

_____

_____

_____

_____

_____

_____

Within my center,

God is ever eager

to embrace, love,

support, guide,

and comfort me

Returning to the Center Within

About this spiritual tip: Within each of us is a center point to which we can return when we feel stressed out and upset, when we need guidance and direction, or when we simply need to feel safe and protected. This safe haven—some call it our soul or spirit—is the unshakable part of our being where our truest and deepest self lives in unity with the Spirit of God.

When we live and act from our center, our Godlike qualities are manifested through our humanity: compassion, empathy, creativity, love, forgiveness, generosity, and so on. When we are not living and acting from our center, fear-driven qualities tend to manifest themselves: excessive regrets about the past, worries about the future, projection, judging, reacting, hoarding, and so on. Becoming off-centered is part of being a flawed human being; becoming centered again is a choice we must make in response to God's continual invitation. God desires that we return inward and open up to the providential gifts that await us: energy, love, support, divine ideas, creativity, forgiveness, consolation, protection, safety, as well as many others. God invites us to come home to the center within and to be at home with God and our deepest self.

Applying and Activating

- Consider visualizing a symbol or a setting to help get in touch with your center, perhaps a warm light, a quiet place by the lake, or a real or imaginary room with a fireplace....
- Close your eyes and with each breath allow yourself to be drawn deeper into your center within.
- Use a short prayer or mantra such as, "Lord, lead me home" or "Spirit of God, center me."
- Visualize your center as being filled with God's unconditional love, protection, peace, or whatever else you need from God.
- Use the following affirmations and truths to help return to your center.

Affirmations and Truths for Returning to the Center Within

When I feel upset and off-center, I will remember to return to my true home within

Before, during, or after any stressful event, I center myself in God's abiding peace

I let go of all that disturbs me and sink into the still, calm, comforting center within

No matter what is happening around me, a safe, impenetrable haven is within me

Within my center, God is ever eager to embrace, love, support, guide, and comfort me

My thoughts, prayers, or affirmations

_____

_____

_____

_____

_____

_____

_____

_____

_____

_____

_____

_____

When my life
becomes
too complex,

naming

helps me
regain simplicity
and clarity

The Power of Naming

About this spiritual tip: One of the many tasks of little children is to learn the names of the people and objects surrounding them. And as they learn these names, they gain the power to express their specific needs and wants, such as "milk," "water," "ball," "Mama."

Because our adult lives are often so complex, the need to name continues to be important. Our inner world is composed of a plethora of thoughts, feelings, hopes, worries, questions, and dreams that are jumbled together in a seemingly indistinguishable conglomeration. However, by simply naming one thought, feeling, hope, or worry, we regain some clarity and power in our lives. We can say aloud to ourselves, "I feel sad about..." Or we can write in our journals, "I am really worried about ..." Or we can share with a friend, "I have been having lots of doubts about God lately..."

Naming reveals what is hidden, clarifies what is obscure, and simplifies what is complex. Naming helps pinpoint what is really going on inside us so that we can care for ourselves, perhaps by talking to someone, seeking help, or praying. Naming reduces the power the unnamed has over us. Naming equips us with personal power and helps to set us free.

Applying and Activating

◆ Name what you are thinking or feeling at this very moment.

◆ Spend some time writing about one or more of the following:
your hopes, fears, worries, dreams, thoughts, or doubts,
and share some of what you named with a trusted friend.

◆ When you are experiencing a painful feeling, name it aloud
and notice if the intensity subsides a bit.

◆ Share with a friend or God some of your inner world each day
or several times a week.

◆ Reflect upon the following affirmations and truths.

Affirmations and Truths about Naming

Naming gives me the clarity and power to consider my options
and to choose wisely

When I name my painful feelings, their intensity is tamed and
they pass through me more quickly

I will name what is *really* going on within me and share myself
with someone I trust

Naming is the first step toward reducing or resolving a problem
or difficulty

When my life becomes too complex, naming helps me regain
simplicity and clarity

Naming reduces the power that the unnamed has over me and
helps to set me free

My thoughts, prayers, or affirmations

_____

_____

_____

_____

_____

_____

_____

_____

_____

_____

_____

_____

_____

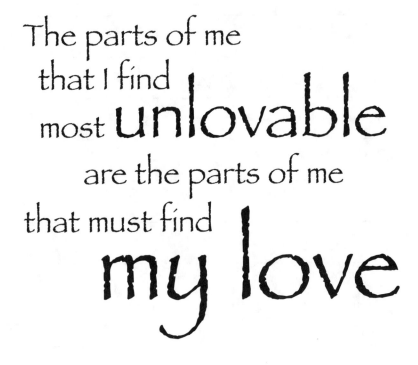

The parts of me
that I find
most unlovable
are the parts of me
that must find
my love

Growing in Self-Love

About this spiritual tip: The triangle of love consists of love for God, love for neighbor, and love for self, and each side is connected to and dependent upon the other two sides. The Bible teaches us that we can't love God if we don't love our neighbor; psychology teaches us that we can't love our neighbor if we don't love ourselves.

While there will always be room for growth and improvement in all three areas, the one that seems to be most underdeveloped—perhaps even neglected—is love for self. Maybe self-love is difficult because we are with ourselves every single moment, and "familiarity breeds contempt." Or, maybe it's hard to love ourselves because the emphasis tends to be on loving God and neighbor. Another factor might be that we find parts of ourselves to be unlovable. Or, maybe self-love is elusive because we don't know how to love ourselves. We do know that love is not primarily a feeling, rather, it is a choice to act in loving ways. So the many ways we show love for others—buying flowers, sending cards, giving a gift, speaking words of support and encouragement—can be imitated in how we love ourselves. We can strengthen self-love by giving to ourselves what we freely give to others.

Applying and Activating

♦ On a scale of one to ten, how would you rate your self-love? Explain.

♦ Discern if there is any aspect of your body or personality that you feel is unlovable, then take some loving actions on your behalf, perhaps by talking to someone, praying, speaking kind words to yourself, etc.

♦ Buy a gift for yourself just because you are you, not because you accomplished anything.

♦ Make a menu of actions from which you can choose specific ways to love yourself. It might include a massage once a month, going for a walk, or buying flowers.

♦ Reflect upon the following affirmations and truths.

Affirmations and Truths for Growing in Self-Love

When I feel most unlovable, I will act with love by doing something kind for myself

As I grow in love for myself, the love I have for my neighbor and for God also grows

The parts of me that I find most unlovable are the parts of me that must find my love

I show love for myself by accepting the love God and others have for me

When I fail to love myself, I will reactivate self-love by forgiving myself and trying again

My thoughts, prayers, or affirmations

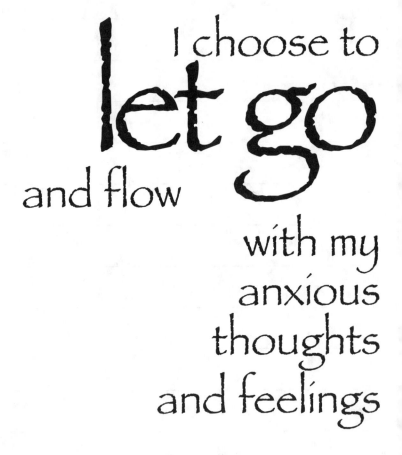

I choose to
let go
and flow
with my
anxious
thoughts
and feelings

Becoming Less Anxious

About this spiritual tip: Free-floating anxiety is a very uncomfortable feeling. For those of us who have suffered anxiety or panic attacks, it is especially painful. The symptoms of anxiety—feeling dis-eased, apprehensive, in danger, like we're falling apart or losing our mind—are so painful that we wouldn't want our worst enemies to suffer them.

Experiencing some anxiety is part of life, but suffering from excessive or crippling anxiety is not something we must endure forever. When caught in anxiety's grip, we tend to feel all alone, but we can take solace in knowing that millions of people have learned how to loosen its hold on them. Instead of feeling ashamed of our anxiety, we need to treat ourselves gently. We must also learn to flow with, rather than fight and resist, anxiety's comings and goings, much like letting a wave wash over us. This is hard to do at first, but it will come more naturally with practice. It is equally important to learn relaxation and meditation techniques, so that we can call upon these tools during our most anxious moments. Finally, we need to remember that dealing with anxiety is not a solo flight; we let God and God-through-others nurture us. Seeking professional help is one way we can do this.

Applying and Activating

- Explore a bookstore or library for a book or tape to help you cope with anxiety and learn relaxation techniques.
- Try writing down some of your anxieties, such as fear of dying or being alone, as a way to lessen their intensity.
- Seek out professional help or a support group.
- Share with someone close to you your struggles with anxiety.
- Use some of the other spiritual tips in this book to help you cope, perhaps #5, 7, 12, 17, 19, or 20.
- Repeat one of the following affirmations or truths over and over.

Affirmations and Truths to Help Reduce Anxious Feelings

I choose to let go and flow with my anxious thoughts and feelings

By regularly practicing relaxation and meditation, my anxiety becomes more irregular

I will guard against shame and secrecy by letting someone know when I am feeling anxious

When I feel anxious, I will be extraordinarily gentle and tender with myself

I do not have to handle anxiety gracefully for no one is judging or condemning me

I celebrate the progress I am making and realize that anxiety does not rule me

My thoughts, prayers, or affirmations

_____

_____

_____

_____

_____

_____

_____

_____

_____

_____

_____

_____

When I lose my way
in prayer,
I trust that God
will help me
find my way
again

Getting Restarted in Prayer

About this spiritual tip: Prayer seems to come quite easily at times and at other times it is incredibly difficult. Because it is not something that can be grasped firmly or controlled, most of us will lose our way in prayer from time to time. (I feel very inept as a pray-er several times each year and plead, "Lord, teach me to pray.") When we are in a slump, we don't have to feel bad about it; instead, we need to keep on "swinging," trusting that God will help us find our prayer-way again.

One way to get unstuck and restarted is to try some different ways of praying. We might try to write some of our prayers, use mantras, spend time in nature, walk, read the psalms, or just be with God in silent love. Another tip for getting restarted in prayer is to pray—and play—with our images of God. We may have limited our images of God and thus unintentionally constricted our prayer lives. By imaging or addressing God as Friend or Mother or Grandmother or Advisor or Coach as well as Father, we can expand our prayer. We might also consider getting help and advice from a spiritual director or advisor or someone else who knows some of the ups and downs and difficulties of prayer.

Applying and Activating

◆ Ask God to teach you how to pray.

◆ Seek help from one of the many books that are available on prayer.

◆ Consider developing a relationship with a spiritual director to discuss your prayer life and other aspects of your life journey.

◆ Read from a daily meditation book so that when prayer is difficult you can still take in some nourishment.

◆ Experiment with some different ways to pray.

◆ When prayer is difficult, let it go for a while rather than trying to force it.

◆ Ponder the following affirmations and truths.

Affirmations and Truths for Getting Restarted in Prayer

When I seem unable to pray, I will seek spiritual nourishment in other creative ways

I will grow in prayer as I grow in my images of God and my practices of prayer

When I lose my way in prayer, I trust that God will help me find my way again

I will make plans to spend time with God in prayer just as I would with a friend

As I practice praying, I am learning to flow with prayer's inevitable ups and downs

When prayer becomes heavy and hard, I will lighten up, play, and pray another day

My thoughts, prayers, or affirmations

_____

_____

_____

_____

_____

_____

_____

_____

_____

_____

_____

_____

_____

It is a SIGN of STRENGTH and WISDOM to ask someone else to HELP me

Asking for Help

About this spiritual tip: Asking for help tends to be a last resort—if even that—for many of us. We sometimes think we should always be able to figure things out for ourselves and handle our own problems. We may operate under the illusion that everyone else is competent and has it all together, so we don't dare risk revealing to the world—which is often just one other struggling person—that we don't have it all together. We compare our insides, our fears and vulnerabilities, to others' outsides, to how they appear to us, which is like comparing bananas to basketballs.

Somewhere along the line, we may have picked up the impossible-to-live-up-to message that we must be competent and strong at all times. Yet, when we risk asking others for help with our struggles and difficulties, their insights and wisdom often enable us to actually go about resolving or reducing the challenges we face. Their distance from our situation provides us with the vision to see our problem more clearly. When we ask God for help, we need to be open to how God often helps us through someone else. Asking for help is essential to our self-care and reveals our wisdom and strength.

Applying and Activating

- Assess the factors that influence your (in)ability to ask for help (fear, embarrassment, etc.).
- Identify the areas of your life for which it would be easiest to ask for help.
- Identify the areas of your life for which it would be hardest to ask for help.
- Assess the factors that contribute to your willingness or unwillingness to ask God for help.
- Identify who would be safest to ask for help at work and in your personal life, and consider doing so when a need arises.
- Read and reflect upon the following affirmations and truths.

Affirmations and Truths About Asking for Help

It is a sign of strength and wisdom to ask someone else to help me

I feel honored when others seek my help, so others probably feel honored when I ask for their help

When I ask God for help, I will be open to the people through whom God works

I will seek help from those who are safe, trustworthy, and respectful

When I ask for help, I am helping someone else know that it is okay to ask for help

My thoughts, prayers, or affirmations

_____

_____

_____

_____

_____

_____

_____

_____

_____

_____

_____

_____

_____

Suggested Reading

Bemis, Judith and Barrada Amr *Embracing the Fear: Learning to Manage Anxiety and Panic Attacks,* Hazelden, 1994.

Bloch, Douglas *Listening to Your Inner Voice: Discover the Truth Within You and Let It Guide Your Way,* Hazelden, 1995.

Cooper, Terry D. *I'm Judgmental You're Judgmental: Healing Our Condemning Attitudes.* Paulist Press, 1999.

Egeberg, Gary *The Pocket Guide to Prayer.* Augsburg Books, 1999.

Froehle, Virginia Ann, R.S.M. *Loving Yourself More: 101 Meditations for Women,* Ave Maria Press, 1993.

Meehan, Bridget Mary and Regina Madonna Oliver *Affirmations from the Heart of God,* Liguori Publications, 1998.

Merrill, Nan C. *Psalms for Praying: An Invitation to Wholeness,* Continuum, 1997.

Miller, D. Patrick *The Book of Practical Faith: A Path to Useful Spirituality,* Henry Holt, 1995.

Nouwen, Henri J.M. *The Inner Voice of Love: A Journey Through Anguish to Freedom,* Doubleday, 1996.

O'Shaughnessy, Mary Michael, O.P. *Feelings and Emotions in Christian Living,* Alba House, 1988.

Padovani, Martin H. *Healing Wounded Emotions: Overcoming Life's Hurts,* Twenty-Third Publications, 1987.

Powers, John *And Grace Will Lead Me Home: A Spiritual Journey.*, McCracken, 1994.

Powers, John *Seeking Inner Peace: The Art of Facing Your Emotions,* Twenty-Third Publications, 1987.

Quillo, Ronald *The Psalms: Prayers of Many Moods,* Paulist Press, 1999.

Redmont, Jane *When in Doubt, Sing: Prayer in Daily Life,* Harper Collins Publishers, 1999.

Richo, David *How to Be an Adult: A Handbook on Psychological and Spiritual Integration,* Paulist Press, 1991.

Thomas, Carolyn *Will the Real God Please Stand Up: Healing Our Dysfunctional Images of God,* Paulist Press, 1991.